Chief Joseph's Own Story And

General Howard's Comment

Chief Joseph

Kessinger Publishing's Rare Reprints

Thousands of Scarce and Hard-to-Find Books on These and other Subjects!

- Americana
- Ancient Mysteries
- Animals
- Anthropology
- Architecture
- Arts
- Astrology
- Bibliographies
- Biographies & Memoirs
- Body, Mind & Spirit
- Business & Investing
- Children & Young Adult
- Collectibles
- Comparative Religions
- Crafts & Hobbies
- Earth Sciences
- Education
- Ephemera
- Fiction
- Folklore
- Geography
- Health & Diet
- History
- Hobbies & Leisure
- Humor
- Illustrated Books
- Language & Culture
- Law
- Life Sciences

- Literature
- Medicine & Pharmacy
- Metaphysical
- Music
- Mystery & Crime
- Mythology
- Natural History
- Outdoor & Nature
- Philosophy
- Poetry
- Political Science
- Science
- Psychiatry & Psychology
- Reference
- Religion & Spiritualism
- Rhetoric
- Sacred Books
- Science Fiction
- Science & Technology
- Self-Help
- Social Sciences
- Symbolism
- Theatre & Drama
- Theology
- Travel & Explorations
- War & Military
- Women
- Yoga
- *Plus Much More!*

We kindly invite you to view our catalog list at:
http://www.kessinger.net

CHAPTER TWO

Chief Joseph's Own Story

With an Introduction by the Rt. Rev. W. H. Hare, D.D.,
Bishop of South Dakota *

I WISH that I had words at command in which to express adequately the interest with which I have read the extraordinary narrative which follows, and which I have the privilege of introducing to the readers of this *Review*. I feel, however, that this apologia is so boldly marked by the charming naïveté and tender pathos which characterizes the red-man, that it needs no introduction, much less any authentication; while in its smothered fire, in its deep sense of eternal righteousness and of present evil, and in its hopeful longings for the coming of a better time, this Indian chief's appeal reminds us of one of the old Hebrew prophets of the days of the Captivity.

I have no special knowledge of the history of the Nez Percés, the Indians whose tale of sorrow Chief Joseph so pathetically tells — my Indian missions lying in a part at the West quite distant from their old home —

* This and the following chapter are taken from *The North American Review* for 1879, by the gracious permission of Messrs. Harper and Brothers, the present publishers of the magazine and the owners of the copyright. — C. T. B.

44

and am not competent to judge their case upon its merits. The chief's narrative is, of course, *ex parte*, and many of his statements would no doubt be ardently disputed. General Howard, for instance, can hardly receive justice at his hands, so well known is he for his friendship to the Indian and for his distinguished success in pacifying some of the most desperate.

It should be remembered, too, in justice to the army, that it is rarely called upon to interfere in Indian affairs until the relations between the Indians and the whites have reached a desperate condition, and when the situation of affairs has become so involved and feeling on both sides runs so high that perhaps only more than human forbearance would attempt to solve the difficulty by disentangling the knot and not by cutting it.

Nevertheless, the chief's narrative is marked by so much candor, and he is so careful to qualify his statements, when qualification seems necessary, that every reader will give him credit for speaking his honest, even should they be thought by some to be mistaken, convictions. The chief, in his treatment of his defense, reminds one of those lawyers of whom we have heard that their splendid success was gained, not by disputation, but simply by their lucid and straightforward statement of their case. That he is something of a strategist as well as an advocate appears from this description of an event which occurred shortly after the breaking out of hostilities: "We crossed over Salmon River, hoping General Howard would follow. We were not disappointed. He did follow us, and we got between him and his supplies, and cut him off for three days." Occasionally the reader comes upon touches of those sentiments and feelings which at once establish a sense of kinship between all who possess them. Witness his description of his desperate attempt to rejoin his wife and children when a sudden dash of General Miles' soldiers had cut the Indian camp in two. . . . "I thought of my wife and children, who were now surrounded by soldiers, and I resolved to go to them. With a prayer in my mouth to the Great Spirit Chief who rules above, I dashed unarmed through the line of soldiers. . . . My clothes were cut to pieces, my horse was wounded, but I was not hurt." And, again, when he speaks of his father's death: "I saw he was dying. I took his hand in mine. He said: 'My son, my body is returning to my mother earth, and my spirit is going very soon to see the Great Spirit Chief. . . . A few more years and the white men will be all around you. They have their eyes on this land. My son, never forget my dying words. This country holds your father's body — never sell the bones of your father and mother.' I pressed my father's hand, and told him I would protect his grave with my life. My father smiled, and passed away to the spirit-land. I buried him in that beautiful valley of Winding Waters. I love that land more than all the rest of the world. A man who would not love his father's grave is worse than a wild animal."

His appeals to the natural rights of man are surprisingly fine, and, however some may despise them as the utterance of an Indian, they are just those which, in our Declaration of Independence, have been most admired. "We are all sprung from a woman," he says, "although we are unlike in many things. You are as you were made, and, as you are made, you can remain. We are just as we were made by the Great Spirit, and you cannot change us; then, why should children of one mother quarrel? Why should one try to cheat another? I do not believe that the Great Spirit Chief gave one kind of men the right to tell another kind of men what they must do."

But I will not detain the readers of the *Review* from the pleasure of perusing for themselves Chief Joseph's statement longer than is necessary to express the hope that those who have time for no more will at least read its closing paragraph, and to remark that the narrative brings clearly out these facts which ought to be regarded as well-recognized principles in dealing with the redman:

1. The folly of any mode of treatment of the Indian which is not based upon a cordial and operative acknowledgment of his rights as our *fellow-man*.

2. The danger of riding roughshod over a people who are capable of high enthusiasm, who know and value their national rights, and are brave enough to defend them.

3. The liability to want of harmony between different departments and different officials of our complex Government, from which it results that, while many promises are made to the Indians, few of them are kept. It is a home-thrust when Chief Joseph says: "The white people have too many chiefs. They do not understand each other. . . . I cannot understand how the Government sends a man out to fight us, as it did General Miles, and then break his word. Such a Government has something wrong about it."

4. The unwisdom, in most cases, in dealing with Indians, of what may be termed *Military short-cuts*, instead of patient discussion, explanations, persuasion, and reasonable concessions.

5. The absence in an Indian tribe of any truly representative body competent to make a treaty which shall be binding upon all the bands. The failure to recognize

this fact has been the source of endless difficulties. Chief Joseph, in this case, did not consider a treaty binding which his band had not agreed to, no matter how many other bands had signed it; and so it has been in many other cases.

6. Indian chiefs, however able and influential, are really without power, and for this reason, as well as others, the Indians, when by the march of events they are brought into intimate relations with the whites, should at the earliest practicable moment be given the support and protection of our Government and of our law; not *local* law, however, which is apt to be the result of *special* legislation adopted solely in the interest of the stronger race. WILLIAM H. HARE.

My friends, I have been asked to show you my heart. I am glad to have a chance to do so. I want the white people to understand my people. Some of you think an Indian is like a wild animal. This is a great mistake. I will tell you all about our people, and then you can judge whether an Indian is a man or not. I believe much trouble and blood would be saved if we opened our hearts more. I will tell you in my way how the Indian sees things. The white man has more words to tell you how they look at him, but it does not require many words to speak the truth. What I have to say will come from my heart, and I will speak with a straight tongue. Ah-cum-kin-i-ma-me-hut (the Great Spirit) is looking at me, and will hear me.

My name is In-mut-too-yah-lat-lat (Thunder-traveling-over-the-mountains). I am chief of the Wal-lam-wat-kin band of Chute-pa-lu, or Nez Percés (nose-pierced Indians). I was born in eastern Oregon, thirty-eight winters ago. My father was chief before me. When

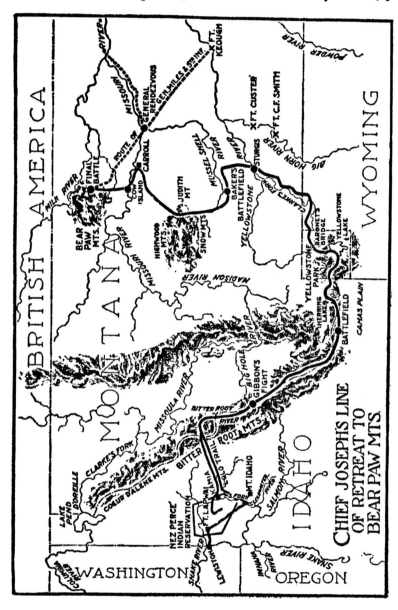

CHIEF JOSEPH'S LINE OF RETREAT TO BEAR PAW MTS.

a young man he was called Joseph by Mr. Spaulding, a missionary. He died a few years ago. There was no stain on his hands of the blood of a white man. He left a good name on the earth. He advised me well for my people.

Our fathers gave us many laws, which they had learned from their fathers. These laws were good. They told us to treat all men as they treated us; that we should never be the first to break a bargain; that it was a disgrace to tell a lie; that we should speak only the truth; that it was a shame for one man to take from another his wife, or his property, without paying for it. We were taught to believe that the Great Spirit sees and hears everything, and that He never forgets; that hereafter He will give every man a spirit-home according to his deserts; if he has been a good man, he will have a good home; if he has been a bad man, he will have a bad home. This I believe, and all my people believe the same.

We did not know there were other people besides the Indian until about one hundred winters ago, when some men with white faces came to our country. They brought many things with them to trade for furs and skins. They brought tobacco, which was new to us. They brought guns with flintstones on them, which frightened our women and children. Our people could not talk with these white-faced men, but they used signs which all people understood. These men were Frenchmen, and they called our people "Nez Percés," because they wore rings in their noses for ornaments. Although very few of our people wear them now, we are still called by the same name. These French trappers said a great many things to our fathers, which have been planted in our hearts. Some were good for us, but some were bad. Our people were divided in opinion about these men. Some thought they taught more bad than good. An

Indian respects a brave man, but he despises a coward.
He loves a straight tongue, but he hates a forked tongue.
The French trappers told us some truths and some lies.

The first white men of your people who came to our
country were named Lewis and Clarke. They also
brought many things that our people had never seen.
They talked straight, and our people gave them a great
feast, as a proof that their hearts were friendly. These
men were very kind. They made presents to our chiefs
and our people made presents to them. We had a great
many horses, of which we gave them what they needed,
and they gave us guns and tobacco in return. All the
Nez Percés made friends with Lewis and Clarke, and
agreed to let them pass through their country, and never
to make war on white men. This promise the Nez Percés
have never broken. No white man can accuse them of
bad faith, and speak with a straight tongue. It has always been the pride of the Nez Percés that they were
the friends of the white men. When my father was a
young man there came to our country a white man (Rev.
Mr. Spaulding) who talked spirit law. He won the af-
fections of our people because he spoke good things
to them. At first he did not say anything about white men
wanting to settle on our lands. Nothing was said about
that until about twenty winters ago when a number
of white people came into our country and built houses
and made farms. At first our people made no complaint.
They thought there was room enough for all to live in
peace, and they were learning many things from the
white men that seemed to be good. But we soon found
that the white men were growing rich very fast, and were
greedy to possess everything the Indian had. My father
was the first to see through the schemes of the white men,
and he warned his tribe to be careful about trading with

them. He had a suspicion of men who seemed so anxious to make money. I was a boy then, but I remember well my father's caution. He had sharper eyes than the rest of our people.

Next there came a white officer (Governor Stevens) who invited all the Nez Percés to a treaty council. After the council was opened he made known his heart. He said there were a great many white people in the country, and many more would come; that he wanted the land marked out so that the Indians and white men could be separated. If they were to live in peace it was necessary, he said, that the Indians should have a country set apart for them, and in that country they must stay. My father, who represented his band, refused to have anything to do with the council, because he wished to be a free man. He claimed that no man owned any part of the earth, and a man could not sell what was not his own.

Mr. Spaulding took hold of my father's arm and said, "Come and sign the treaty." My father pushed him away and said: "Why do you ask me to sign away my country? It is your business to talk to us about spirit matters, and not to talk to us about parting with our land." Governor Stevens urged my father to sign his treaty, but he refused. "I will not sign your paper," he said, "you go where you please, so do I: you are not a child, I am no child; I can think for myself. No man can think for me. I have no other home than this. I will not give it up to any man. My people would have no home. Take away your paper. I will not touch it with my hand."

My father left the council. Some of the chiefs of the other bands of the Nez Percés signed the treaty, and then Governor Stevens gave them presents of blankets. My father cautioned his people to take no presents, for "after awhile," he said, "they will claim that you accepted pay for your country." Since that time four bands of the Nez Percés have received annuities from the United States. My father was invited to many councils, and they tried hard to make him sign the treaty, but he was firm as the rock, and would not sign away his home. His refusal caused a difference among the Nez Percés.

Eight years later (1863) was the next treaty council. A chief called Lawyer, because he was a great talker, took the lead in this council, and sold nearly all of the Nez Percés country. My father was not there. He said to me: "When you go into council with the white man, always remember your country. Do not give it away. The white man will cheat you out of your home. I have taken no pay from the United States. I have never sold our land." In this treaty Lawyer acted without authority from our band. He had no right to sell the Wallowa (*winding water*) country. That had always belonged to my father's own people, and the other bands had never disputed our right to it. No other Indians ever claimed Wallowa.

In order to have all people understand how much land we owned, my father planted poles around it and said:

"Inside is the home of my people — the white man may take the land outside. Inside this boundary all our people were born. It circles around the graves of our fathers, and we will never give up these graves to any man."

The United States claimed they had bought all the Nez Percés country outside the Lapwai Reservation, from Lawyer and other chiefs, but we continued to live on this land in peace until eight years ago, when white men began to come inside the bounds my father had set. We warned them against this great wrong, but they would not leave our land, and some bad blood was raised. The white man represented that we were going upon the war-path. They reported many things that were false.

The United States Government again asked for a treaty council. My father had become blind and feeble. He could no longer speak for his people. It was then I took my father's place as chief. In this council I made my first speech to white men. I said to the agent who held the council:

"I did not want to come to this council, but I came hoping that we could save blood. The white man has no right to come here and take our country. We have never accepted presents from the Government. Neither Lawyer nor any other chief had authority to sell this land. It has always belonged to my people. It came unclouded to them from our fathers, and we will defend this land as long as a drop of Indian blood warms the hearts of our men."

The agent said he had orders, from the Great White Chief at Washington, for us to go upon the Lapwai Reservation, and that if we obeyed he would help us in many ways. "You *must* move to the agency," he said. I answered him: "I will not. I do not need your help; we have plenty, and we are contented and happy if the white man will let us alone. The reservation is too small for so many people with all their stock. You can keep your presents; we can go to your towns and pay for all we need; we have plenty of horses and cattle to sell, and we won't have any help from you; we are free now; we can go where we please. Our fathers were born here. Here they lived, here they died, here are their

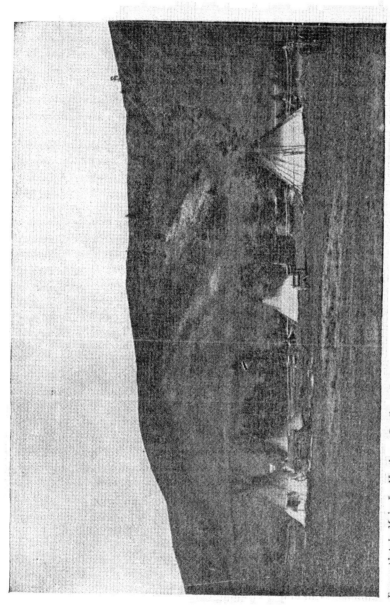

From a photo by Major Lee Moorhouse, Pendleton, Oregon

Last Home of Chief Joseph, where he Dropped Dead at the Camp Fire, September, 1904—Nespelum. Colville Reservation of Moses Indians, Washington State

From the collection of J. W. Redington

Colonel W. R. Parnell,
U. S. A., retired

First Lieutenant Robert H
Fletcher, U. S. A., retired

Brigadier-General David
Perry, U. S. A., retired

Major J G. Trimble, U. S.A.,
retired

Distinguished Officers of the Nez Perce War

graves. We will never leave them." The agent went away, and we had peace for awhile.

Soon after this my father sent for me. I saw he was dying. I took his hand in mine. He said: "My son, my body is returning to my mother earth, and my spirit is going very soon to see the Great Spirit Chief. When I am gone, think of your country. You are the chief of these people. They look to you to guide them. Always remember that your father never sold his country. You must stop your ears whenever you are asked to sign a treaty selling your home. A few years more, and white men will be all around you. They have their eyes on this land. My son, never forget my dying words. This country holds your father's body. Never sell the bones of your father and your mother." I pressed my father's hand and told him that I would protect his grave with my life. My father smiled and passed away to the spirit-land.

I buried him in that beautiful valley of winding waters. I love that land more than all the rest of the world. A man who would not love his father's grave is worse than a wild animal.

For a short time we lived quietly. But this could not last. White men had found gold in the mountains around the land of the winding water. They stole a great many horses from us, and we could not get them back because we were Indians. The white men told lies for each other. They drove off a great many of our cattle. Some white men branded our young cattle so they could claim them. We had no friend who would plead our cause before the law councils. It seemed to me that some of the white men in Wallowa were doing these things on purpose to get up a war. They knew that we were not strong enough to fight them. I labored hard to avoid trouble and bloodshed. We gave up some of our country to the white men, thinking that then we could have peace. We were mistaken. The white man would not let us alone. We could have avenged our wrongs many times, but we did not. Whenever the Government has asked us to help them against other Indians, we have never refused. When the white men were few and we were strong we could have killed them off, but the Nez Percés wished to live at peace.

If we have not done so, we have not been to blame. I believe that the old treaty has never been correctly reported. If we ever owned the land we own it still, for we never sold it. In the treaty councils the commissioners have claimed that our country had been sold to the Government. Suppose a white man should come to me and say, "Joseph, I like your horses, and I want to buy them." I say to him, "No, my horses suit me, I will not sell them." Then he goes to my neighbor, and says to him: "Joseph has some good horses. I want to buy them, but he refuses to sell." My neighbor answers, "Pay me the money, and I will sell you Joseph's horses." The white man returns to me and says, "Joseph, I have bought your horses, and you must let me have them." If we sold our lands to the Government, this is the way they were bought.

On account of the treaty made by the other bands of Nez Percés, the white men claimed my lands. We were troubled greatly by white men crowding over the line. Some of these were good men, and we lived on peaceful terms with them, but they were not all good.

Nearly every year the agent came over from Lapwai and ordered us on to the reservation. We always replied that we were satisfied to live in Wallowa. We were careful to refuse the presents or annuities which he offered.

Through all the years since the white man came to Wallowa we have been threatened and taunted by them and the treaty Nez Percés. They have given us no rest. We have had a few good friends among white men, and they have always advised my people to bear these taunts without fighting. Our young men were quick-tempered, and I have had great trouble in keeping them from doing rash things. I have carried a heavy load on my back ever since I was a boy. I learned then that we were but few, while the white men were many, and that we could not hold our own with them. We were like deer. They were like grizzly bears. We had a small country. Their country was large. We were contented to let things remain as the Great Spirit Chief made them. They were not; and would change the rivers and mountains if they did not suit them.

Year after year we have been threatened, but no war was made upon my people until General Howard came to our country two years ago and told us that he was the white war-chief of all that country. He said: "I have a great many soldiers at my back. I am going to bring them up here, and then I will talk to you again. I will not let white men laugh at me the next time I come. The country belongs to the Government, and I intend to make you go upon the reservation."

I remonstrated with him against bringing more soldiers to the Nez Percés country. He had one house full of troops all the time at Fort Lapwai.

The next spring the agent at Umatilla Agency sent an Indian runner to tell me to meet General Howard at Walla Walla. I could not go myself, but I sent my brother and five other head men to meet him, and they had a long talk.

General Howard said: "You have talked straight, and

it is all right. You can stay at Wallowa." He insisted
that my brother and his company should go with him
to Fort Lapwai. When the party arrived there General
Howard sent out runners and called all the Indians to a
grand council. I was in that council. I said to General
Howard, "We are ready to listen." He answered that
he would not talk then, but would hold a council next
day, when he would talk plainly. I said to General Howard: "I am ready to talk to-day. I have been in a great
many councils, but I am no wiser. We are all sprung
from a woman, although we are unlike in many things.
We cannot be made over again. You are as you were
made, and as you were made you can remain. We are
just as we were made by the Great Spirit, and you cannot change us; then why should children of one mother
and one father quarrel? — why should one try to cheat
the other? I do not believe that the Great Spirit Chief
gave one kind of men the right to tell another kind of
men what they must do."

General Howard replied: "You deny my authority,
do you? You want to dictate to me, do you?"

Then one of my chiefs — Too-hool-hool-suit — rose
in the council and said to General Howard: "The Great
Spirit Chief made the world as it is, and as He wanted it,
and He made a part of it for us to live upon. I do not see
where you get authority to say that we shall not live
where He placed us."

General Howard lost his temper and said: "Shut up!
I don't want to hear any more of such talk. The law
says you shall go upon the reservation to live, and I want
you to do so, but you persist in disobeying the law"
(meaning the treaty). "If you do not move, I will take
the matter into my own hand, and make you suffer for
your disobedience."

Too-hool-hool-suit answered: "Who are you, that you ask us to talk, and then tell me I shan't talk? Are you the Great Spirit? Did you make the world? Did you make the sun? Did you make the rivers to run for us to drink? Did you make the grass to grow? Did you make all these things that you talk to us as though we were boys? If you did, then you have the right to talk as you do."

General Howard replied: "You are an impudent fellow, and I will put you in the guard-house," and then ordered a soldier to arrest him.

Too-hool-hool-suit made no resistance. He asked General Howard: "Is this your order? I don't care. I have expressed my heart to you. I have nothing to take back. I have spoken for my country. You can arrest me, but you cannot change me or make me take back what I have said."

The soldiers came forward and seized my friend and took him to the guard-house. My men whispered among themselves whether they would let this thing be done. I counseled them to submit. I knew if we resisted that all the white men present, including General Howard, would be killed in a moment, and we would be blamed. If I had said nothing, General Howard would never have given an unjust order against my men. I saw the danger and while they dragged Too-hool-hool-suit to prison, I arose and said: "*I am going to talk now. I don't care whether you arrest me or not.*" I turned to my people and said: "The arrest of Too-hool-hool-suit was wrong, but we will not resent the insult. We were invited to this council to express our hearts, and we have done so." Too-hool-hool-suit was prisoner for five days before he was released.

The council broke up that day. On the next morning

General Howard came to my lodge, and invited me to go with him and White Bird and Looking Glass, to look for land for my people. As we rode along we came to some good land that was already occupied by Indians and white people. General Howard, pointing to this land, said: "If you will come on to the reservation, I will give you these lands and move these people off."

I replied: "No. It would be wrong to disturb these people. I have no right to take their homes. I have never taken what did not belong to me. I will not now."

We rode all day upon the reservation, and found no good land unoccupied. I have been informed by men who do not lie that General Howard sent a letter that night telling the soldiers at Walla Walla to go to Wallowa Valley, and drive us out upon our return home.

In the council next day General Howard informed us in a haughty spirit that he would give my people *thirty days* to go back home, collect all their stock, and move on to the reservation, saying, "If you are not here in that time, I shall consider that you want to fight, and will send my soldiers to drive you on."

I said: "War can be avoided and it ought to be avoided. I want no war. My people have always been the friends of the white man. Why are you in such a hurry ? I cannot get ready to move in thirty days. Our stock is scattered, and Snake River is very high. Let us wait until fall, then the river will be low. We want time to hunt our stock and gather our supplies for the winter."

General Howard replied, "If you let the time run over one day, the soldiers will be there to drive you on to the reservation, and all your cattle and horses outside of the reservation at that time will fall into the hands of the white men."

I knew I had never sold my country, and that I had

no land in Lapwai; but I did not want bloodshed. I did not want my people killed. I did not want anybody killed. Some of my people had been murdered by white men, and the white murderers were never punished for it. I told General Howard about this, and again said I wanted no war. I wanted the people who live upon the lands I was to occupy at Lapwai to have time to gather their harvest.

I said in my heart that, rather than have war I would give up my country. I would rather give up my father's grave. I would give up everything rather than have the blood of white men upon the hands of my people.

General Howard refused to allow me more than thirty days to move my people and their stock. I am sure that he began to prepare for war at once.

When I returned to Wallowa I found my people very much excited upon discovering that the soldiers were already in the Wallowa Valley. We held a council, and decided to move immediately to avoid bloodshed.

Too-hool-hool-suit, who felt outraged by his imprisonment, talked for war, and made many of my young men willing to fight rather than be driven like dogs from the land where they were born. He declared that blood alone would wash out the disgrace General Howard had put upon him. It required a strong heart to stand up against such talk, but I urged my people to be quiet, and not to begin a war.

We gathered all the stock we could find, and made an attempt to move. We left many of our horses and cattle in Wallowa, and we lost several hundred in crossing the river. All my people succeeded in getting across in safety. Many of the Nez Percés came together in Rocky Cañon to hold a grand council. I went with all my people. This council lasted ten days. There was a great deal of war talk and a great deal of excitement. There was one young brave present whose father had been killed by a white man five years before. This man's blood was bad against white men and he left the council calling for revenge.

Again I counseled peace, and I thought the danger was past We had not complied with General Howard's order because we could not, but we intended to do so as soon as possible. I was leaving the council to kill beef for my family, when news came that the young man whose father had been killed had gone out with several hot-blooded young braves and killed four white men. He rode up to the council and shouted: "Why do you sit here like women? The war has begun already." I was deeply grieved. All the lodges were moved except my brother's and my own. I saw clearly that the war was upon us when I learned that my young men had been secretly buying ammunition. I heard then that Too-hool-hool-suit, who had been imprisoned by General Howard, had succeeded in organizing a war party. I knew that their acts would involve all my people. I saw that the war could not then be prevented. The time had passed. I counseled peace from the beginning. I knew that we were too weak to fight the United States. We had many grievances, but I knew that war would bring more. We had good white friends, who advised us against taking the war-path. My friend and brother, Mr. Chapman, who has been with us since the surrender, told us just how the war would end. Mr. Chapman took sides against us and helped General Howard. I do not blame him for doing so. He tried hard to prevent bloodshed. We hoped the white settlers would not join the soldiers. Before the war commenced we had discussed this matter all over, and many of my people were in favor of warning them that if they took no part against us they should not be molested in the event of war being begun by General Howard. This plan was voted down in the war-council.

There were bad men among my people who had quarreled with white men, and they talked of their wrongs until they roused all the bad hearts in the council. Still I could not believe that they would begin the war. I know that my young men did a great wrong, but I ask, Who was first to blame? They had been insulted a thousand times; their fathers and brothers had been killed; their mothers and wives had been disgraced; they had been driven to madness by the whiskey sold to them by the white men; they had been told by General Howard that all their horses and cattle which they had been unable to drive out of Wallowa were to fall into the hands of white men; and, added to all this, they were homeless and desperate.

I would have given my own life if I could have undone the killing of white men by my people. I blame my young men and I blame the white men. I blame General Howard for not giving my people time to get their stock away from Wallowa. I do not acknowledge that he had the right to order me to leave Wallowa at any time. I deny that either my father or myself ever sold that land. It is still our land. It may never again be our home, but my father sleeps there, and I love it as I love my mother. I left there, hoping to avoid bloodshed.

If General Howard had given me plenty of time to gather up my stock, and treated Too-hool-hool-suit as a man should be treated, there *would have been no war.* My friends among white men have blamed me for the war. I am not to blame. When my young men began the killing, my heart was hurt. Although I did not justify them, I remembered all the insults I had endured, and my blood was on fire. Still I would have taken my people to the buffalo country without fighting, if possible.

I could see no other way to avoid a war. We moved over to White Bird Creek, sixteen miles away, and there encamped, intending to collect our stock before leaving; but the soldiers attacked us and the first battle was fought. We numbered in that battle sixty men, and the soldiers a hundred. The fight lasted but a few minutes, when the soldiers retreated before us for twelve miles. They lost thirty-three killed, and had seven wounded. When an Indian fights, he only shoots to kill; but soldiers shoot at random. None of the soldiers were scalped. We do not believe in scalping, nor in killing wounded men. Soldiers do not kill many Indians unless they are wounded and left upon the battle-field. Then they kill Indians.

Seven days after the first battle General Howard arrived in the Nez Percés country, bringing seven hundred more soldiers. It was now war in earnest. We crossed over Salmon River, hoping General Howard would follow. We were not disappointed. He did follow us, and we got between him and his supplies, and cut him off for three days. He sent out two companies to open the way. We attacked them, killing one officer, two guides, and ten men.

We withdrew, hoping the soldiers would follow, but they had got fighting enough for that day. They intrenched themselves, and next day we attacked again. The battle lasted all day, and was renewed next morning. We killed four and wounded seven or eight.

About this time General Howard found out that we were in his rear. Five days later he attacked us with three hundred and fifty soldiers and settlers. We had two hundred and fifty warriors. The fight lasted twenty-seven hours. We lost four killed and several wounded. General Howard's loss was twenty-nine men killed and sixty wounded.

The following day the soldiers charged upon us, and we retreated with our families and stock a few miles, leaving eighty lodges to fall into General Howard's hands.

Finding that we were outnumbered, we retreated to Bitter Root Valley. Here another body of soldiers came upon us and demanded our surrender. We refused. They said, "You cannot get by us." We answered, "We are going by you without fighting if you will let us, but we are going by you anyhow." We then made a treaty with these soldiers. We agreed not to molest any one and they agreed that we might pass through the Bitter Root country in peace. We bought provisions and traded stock with white men there.

We understood that there was to be no war. We intended to go peaceably to the buffalo country, and leave the question of returning to our country to be settled afterward.

With this understanding we traveled on for four days, and, thinking that the trouble was all over, we stopped and prepared tent-poles to take with us. We started again, and at the end of two days we saw three white men passing our camp. Thinking that peace had been made, we did not molest them. We could have killed, or taken them prisoners, but we did not suspect them of being spies, which they were.

That night the soldiers surrounded our camp. About daybreak one of my men went out to look after his horses. The soldiers saw him and shot him down like a coyote. I have since learned that these soldiers were not those we had left behind. They had come upon us from another direction. The new white war-chief's name was Gibbon. He charged upon us while some of my people were still asleep. We had a hard fight. Some of my men crept around and attacked the soldiers from the rear. In this battle we lost nearly all our lodges, but we finally drove General Gibbon back.

Finding that he was not able to capture us, he sent to his camp a few miles away for his big guns (cannons), but my men had captured them and all the ammunition. We damaged the big guns all we could, and carried away the powder and lead. In the fight with General Gibbon we lost fifty women and children and thirty fighting men. We remained long enough to bury our dead. The Nez Percés never make war on women and children; we could have killed a great many women and children while the war lasted, but we would feel ashamed to do so cowardly an act.

We never scalp our enemies, but when General Howard came up and joined General Gibbon, their Indian scouts dug up our dead and scalped them. I have been told that General Howard did not order this great shame to be done.

We retreated as rapidly as we could toward the buffalo country. After six days General Howard came close to us, and we went out and attacked him, and captured nearly all his horses and mules (about two hundred and fifty head). We then marched on to the Yellowstone Basin.

On the way we captured one white man and two white women. We released them at the end of three days. They were treated kindly. The women were not insulted. Can the white soldiers tell me of one time when Indian women were taken prisoners, and held three days and then released without being insulted ? Were the Nez

Percés women who fell into the hands of General Howard's soldiers treated with as much respect? I deny that a Nez Percé was ever guilty of such a crime.

A few days later we captured two more white men. One of them stole a horse and escaped. We gave the other a poor horse and told him that he was free.

Nine days' march brought us to the mouth of Clarke's Fork of the Yellowstone. We did not know what had become of General Howard, but we supposed that he had sent for more horses and mules. He did not come up, but another new war-chief (General Sturgis) attacked us. We held him in check while we moved all our women and children and stock out of danger, leaving a few men to cover our retreat.

Several days passed, and we heard nothing of General Howard, or Gibbon, or Sturgis. We had repulsed each in turn, and began to feel secure, when another army, under General Miles, struck us. This was the fourth army, each of which outnumbered our fighting force, that we had encountered within sixty days.

We had no knowledge of General Miles' army until a short time before he made a charge upon us, cutting our camp in two, and capturing nearly all of our horses. About seventy men, myself among them, were cut off. My little daughter, twelve years of age, was with me. I gave her a rope, and told her to catch a horse and join the others who were cut off from the camp. I have not seen her since, but I have learned that she is alive and well.

I thought of my wife and children, who were now surrounded by soldiers, and I resolved to go to them or die. With a prayer in my mouth to the Great Spirit Chief who rules above, I dashed unarmed through the line of soldiers. It seemed to me that there were guns on every side, before and behind me. My clothes were cut to pieces and my horse was wounded, but I was not hurt. As I reached the door of my lodge, my wife handed me my rifle, saying: "Here's your gun. Fight!"

The soldiers kept up a continuous fire. Six of my men were killed in one spot near me. Ten or twelve soldiers charged into our camp and got possession of two lodges, killing three Nez Percés and losing three of their men, who fell inside our lines. I called my men to drive them back. We fought at close range, not more than twenty steps apart, and drove the soldiers back upon their main line, leaving their dead in our hands. We secured their arms and ammunition. We lost, the first day and night, eighteen men and three women. General Miles lost twenty-six killed and forty wounded. The following day General Miles sent a messenger into my camp under protection of a white flag. I sent my friend Yellow Bull to meet him.

Yellow Bull understood the messenger to say that General Miles wished me to consider the situation; that he did not want to kill my people unnecessarily. Yellow Bull understood this to be a demand for me to surrender and save blood. Upon reporting this message to me, Yellow Bull said he wondered whether General Miles was in earnest. I sent him back with my answer, that I had not made up my mind, but would think about it and send word soon. A little later he sent some Cheyenne scouts with another message. I went out to meet them. They said they believed that General Miles was sincere and really wanted peace. I walked on to General Miles' tent. He met me and we shook hands. He said, "Come, let us sit down by the fire and talk this matter over." I remained with him all night; next morning, Yellow Bull came over to see if I was alive, and why I did not return.

General Miles would not let me leave the tent to see my friend alone.

Yellow Bull said to me: "They have got you in their power, and I am afraid they will never let you go again. I have an officer in our camp, and I will hold him until they let you go free."

I said: "I do not know what they mean to do with me, but if they kill me you must not kill the officer. It will do no good to avenge my death by killing him."

Yellow Bull returned to my camp. I did not make any agreement that day with General Miles. The battle was renewed while I was with him. I was very anxious about my people. I knew that we were near Sitting Bull's camp in King George's land, and I thought maybe the Nez Percés who had escaped would return with assistance. No great damage was done to either party during the night.

On the following morning I returned to my camp by agreement, meeting the officer who had been held a prisoner in my camp at the flag of truce. My people were divided about surrendering. We could have escaped from Bear Paw Mountain if we had left our wounded, old women, and children behind. We were unwilling to do this. We had never heard of a wounded Indian recovering while in the hands of white men.

On the evening of the fourth day, General Howard came in with a small escort, together with my friend Chapman. We could now talk understandingly. General Miles said to me in plain words, "If you will come out and give up your arms, I will spare your lives and send you back to the reservation." I do not know what passed between General Miles and General Howard.

I could not bear to see my wounded men and women suffer any longer; we had lost enough already. General

Miles had promised that we might return to our country with what stock we had left. I thought we could start again. I believed General Miles, *or I never would have surrendered.* I have heard that he has been censured for making the promise to return us to Lapwai. He could not have made any other terms with me at that time. I would have held him in check until my friends came to my assistance, and then neither of the generals nor their soldiers would have ever left Bear Paw Mountain alive.

On the fifth day I went to General Miles and gave up my gun, and said, "From where the sun now stands I will fight no more." My people needed rest — we wanted peace.

I was told we could go with General Miles to Tongue River and stay there until spring, when we would be sent back to our country. Finally it was decided that we were to be taken to Tongue River. We had nothing to say about it. After our arrival at Tongue River, General Miles received orders to take us to Bismarck. The reason given was, that subsistence would be cheaper there.

General Miles was opposed to this order. He said: "You must not blame me. I have endeavored to keep my word, but the chief who is over me has given the order, and I must obey it or resign. That would do you no good. Some other officer would carry out the order."

I believe General Miles would have kept his word if he could have done so. I do not blame him for what we have suffered since the surrender. I do not know who is to blame. We gave up all our horses — over eleven hundred — and all our saddles — over one hundred — and we have not heard from them since. Somebody has got our horses.

General Miles turned my people over to another soldier, and we were taken to Bismarck. Captain Johnson, who now had charge of us, received an order to take us to Fort Leavenworth. At Leavenworth we were placed in on a low river bottom, with no water except river water to drink and cook with. We had always lived in a healthy country, where the mountains were high and the water was cold and clear. Many of our people sickened and died, and we buried them in this strange land.* I cannot tell how much my heart suffered for my people while at Leavenworth. The Great Spirit Chief who rules above seemed to be looking some other way, and did not see what was being done to my people.

During the hot days (July, 1878) we received notice that we were to be moved farther away from our own country. We were not asked if we were willing to go. We were ordered to get into the railroad-cars. Three of my people died on the way to Baxter Springs. It was worse to die there than to die fighting in the mountains.

We were moved from Baxter Springs (Kansas) to the Indian Territory and set down without our lodges. We had but little medicine and we were nearly all sick. Seventy of my people have died since we moved there.

We have had a great many visitors who have talked many ways. Some of the chiefs (General Fish and Colonel Stickney) from Washington came to see us, and selected land for us to live upon. We have not moved to that land, for it is not a good place to live.

The Commissioner Chief (E. A. Hayt) came to see us. I told him, as I told every one, that I expected General Miles' word would be carried out. He said it "could not be done; that white men now lived in my country and all the land was taken up; that, if I returned to Wallowa, I could not live in peace; that law-papers were out against my young men who began the war, and that

* I can corroborate this.   I saw them there often.—C. T. B.

the Government could not protect my people." This talk fell like a heavy stone upon my heart. I saw that I could not gain anything by talking to him. Other law chiefs (Congressional Committee) came to see us and said they would help me to get a healthy country. I did not know whom to believe. The white people have too many chiefs. They do not understand each other. They do not talk alike.

The Commissioner Chief (Mr. Hayt) invited me to go with him and hunt for a better home than we have now. I like the land we found (west of the Osage Reservation) better than any place I have seen in that country; but it is not a healthy land. There are no mountains and rivers. The water is warm. It is not a good country for stock. I do not believe my people can live there. I am afraid they will all die. The Indians who occupy that country are dying off. I promised Chief Hayt to go there, and do the best I could until the Government got ready to make good General Miles' word. I was not satisfied, but I could not help myself.

Then the Inspector Chief (General McNiel) came to my camp and we had a long talk. He said I ought to have a home in the mountain country north, and that he would write a letter to the Great Chief in Washington. Again the hope of seeing the mountains of Idaho and Oregon grew up in my heart.

At last I was granted permission to come to Washington and bring my friend Yellow Bull and our interpreter with me. I am glad we came. I have shaken hands with a great many friends, but there are some things I want to know which no one seems able to explain. I cannot understand how the Government sends a man out to fight us, as it did General Miles, and then breaks his word. Such a Government has something wrong about it. I cannot understand why so many chiefs are allowed to talk so many different ways, and promise so many different things. I have seen the Great Father Chief (the President); the next Great Chief (Secretary of the Interior); the Commissioner Chief (Hayt); the Law Chief (General Butler), and many other law chiefs (Congressmen), and they all say they are my friends, and that I shall have justice, but while their mouths all talk right I do not understand why nothing is done for my people. I have heard talk and talk, but nothing is done. Good words do not last long until they amount to something. Words do not pay for my dead people. They do not pay for my country, now overrun by white men. They do not protect my father's grave. They do not pay for my horses and cattle. Good words will not give me back my children. Good words will not make good the promise of your War Chief, General Miles. Good words will not give my people good health and stop them from dying. Good words will not get my people a home where they can live in peace and take care of themselves. I am tired of talk that comes to nothing. It makes my heart sick when I remember all the good words and all the broken promises. There has been too much talking by men who had no right to talk. Too many misrepresentations have been made, too many misunderstandings have come up between the white men about the Indians. If the white man wants to live in peace with the Indian he can live in peace. There need be no trouble. Treat all men alike. Give them all the same law. Give them all an even chance to live and grow. All men were made by the same Great Spirit Chief. They are all brothers. The earth is the mother of all people, and all people should have equal rights upon it. You might as well expect the rivers to run backward as that any man who was born a free man should be contented penned up and denied liberty to go where he pleases. If you tie a horse to a stake, do you expect he will grow fat? If you pen an Indian up on a small spot of earth, and compel him to stay there, he will not be contented nor will he grow and prosper. I have asked some of the great white chiefs where they get their authority to say to the Indian that he shall stay in one place, while he sees white men going where they please. They cannot tell me.

I only ask of the Government to be treated as all other men are treated. If I cannot go to my own home, let me have a home in some country where my people will not die so fast. I would like to go to Bitter Root Valley. There my people would be healthy; where they are now they are dying. Three have died since I left my camp to come to Washington.

When I think of our condition my heart is heavy. I see men of my race treated as outlaws and driven from country to country, or shot down like animals.

I know that my race must change. We cannot hold our own with the white men as we are. We only ask an even chance to live as other men live. We ask to be recognized as men. We ask that the same law shall work alike on all men. If the Indian breaks the law, punish him by the law. If the white man breaks the law, punish him also.

Let me be a free man — free to travel, free to stop, free to work, free to trade, where I choose, free to choose my own teachers, free to follow the religion of my fathers, free to think and talk and act for myself — and I will obey every law, or submit to the penalty.

Whenever the white man treats the Indian as they treat each other, then we shall have no more wars. We shall be all alike — brothers of one father and one mother, with one sky above us and one country around us, and one government for all. Then the Great Spirit Chief who rules above will smile upon this land, and send rain to wash out the bloody spots made by brothers' hands upon the face of the earth. For this time the Indian race are waiting and praying. I hope that no more groans of wounded men and women will ever go to the ear of the Great Spirit Chief above, and that all people may be one people.

In-mut-too-vah-lat-lat has spoken for his people.

YOUNG JOSEPH.

CHAPTER THREE

General Howard's Comment on Joseph's Narrative

By Maj.-Gen. O. O. Howard, United States Army
(Retired)

ON reading in the *North American Review*
for April the article entitled "An Indian's
View of Indian Affairs," I was so pleased
with Joseph's statement — necessarily *ex
parte* though it was, and naturally inspired by resent-
ment toward me as a supposed enemy — that at first I
had no purpose of making a rejoinder. But when I saw
in the *Army and Navy Journal* long passages quoted
from Joseph's tale, which appeared to reflect unfavor-
ably upon my official conduct, to lay upon me the blame
of the atrocious murders committed by the Indians, and
to convict me of glaring faults where I had deemed myself worthy only of commendation, I addressed to the
editor of that journal a communication (which has
been published) correcting misstatements, and briefly
setting forth the facts of the case.

If I had had the power and management entirely in
my hands, I believe I could have healed that old sore,
and established peace and amity with Joseph's Indians.
It could only have been done, first, by a retrocession of
Wallowa (already belonging to Oregon) to the United

tation, and give law to us. The land is ours, and not yours."

Joseph's pictures of frontier troubles between whites and Indians are graphic and true. The killing of a member of his tribe by a white man he refers to. This came near causing an outbreak. The troops intervened between the settlers and the Indians, and the latter quieted down. But the slow process of the civil law, and the prejudice against Indians in all frontier courts, almost invariably prevent the punishment of crimes against Indians. I did what I could to further the ends of justice, in bringing the guilty to trial; but my efforts in this case resulted in nothing. The Indian has a complaint against us (army and agents), because we can and do punish *him*, but do not and cannot punish *white men* who steal the Indian's property and take life.

"But no war was made on my people until General Howard came to our country two years ago," etc. This has all the summary brevity of Shakspere's history, but is not more accurate. The facts are, that I had been in command of the department since the fall of 1874, and had many dealings with Joseph and his people.

The "non-treaties" became suspiciously restless during the Modoc troubles. This was quieted by my worthy predecessor, by sending a considerable force among them just after the Modoc War.

General Davis, speaking of a large gathering of Indians that boded difficulty at the Wee-ipe, says: "The troops did not interfere with the council (twelve hundred Indians), but their presence there for about ten days had the effect to disperse it. General dissatisfaction, however, seemed to prevail among the 'non-treaty Nez Percés.' This was particularly the case with Joseph's band, the claimants of Wallowa Valley."

Again, the *same year* (1874), these Indians were so restless and threatening that Maj. John Green, First Cavalry, was sent to Wallowa Valley with two companies, and remained till the Indians left for their winter quarters.

The next year (1875), I say in my report: "The troubles at Lapwai and Wallowa Valley have not thus far resulted in bloodshed; but it has been prevented by great carefulness and provision on the part of the Government agents."

The year following (1876), my report goes into the trouble again at length, mentioning the grave fact that "an Indian was killed by a white man in a dispute concerning some stock," and winds up with these words: "And renew my recommendation of a commission to hear and settle the whole matter, before war is even thought of." The commission was at last ordered, but not until after blood had been shed — not till after the Indians had stood up in battle array against armed citizens in Wallowa; and a conflict was averted only by the intervention of regular troops. The commission came, held its memorable sessions at Lapwai in November of 1876, and labored hard and long to get the consent of the disaffected "non-treaty Indians" to some measures of adjustment.

Here are a few of the facts developed by this commission: "The Dreamers, among other pernicious doctrines, teach that the earth being created by God complete, should not be disturbed by man; and that any cultivation of the soil or other improvements to interfere with its natural productions; any voluntary submission to the control of the Government; any improvement in the way of schools, churches, etc., are crimes from which they shrink. This fanaticism is kept alive by the superstition of these Dreamers, who industriously teach that if they continue steadfast in their present belief a leader will be raised up (in the East), who will restore all the dead Indians to life, who will unite with them in expelling the whites from their country, when they will again enter upon and repossess the lands of their ancestors.

"Influenced by such belief, Joseph and his band firmly declined to enter into any negotiations, or make any arrangements that looked to a final settlement of the question pending between him and the Government . . . yet, in view of the fact that these Indians do not claim simply this (rights of occupancy), but set up an absolute title to the lands, an absolute and independent sovereignty, and refuse even to be limited in their claim and control, necessity, humanity, and good sense constrain the Government to set metes and bounds and give regulations to these non-treaty Indians. . . . And if the principle usually applied by the Government, of holding that the Indians with whom they have treaties are bound by majorities, is here applied, Joseph should be required to live within the limits of the present reservation."

The commission, though firm and strong in the expression of its opinion, was very patient with and kind to the Indians. I was a member of this commission, and earnestly desired peace. I took Joseph's brother by himself and showed him how much it would be for the Indians' advantage to come to some settlement and spent a long time in giving him and his brother, in the kindest manner, the benefit of my counsel. They appeared at one time almost on the point of yielding, but bad advice intervened to renew the Dreamer sophistry. The commission promised that they should annually visit Wallowa, and so recommended. But here are a few closing words: "If these Indians overrun land belonging to the whites and commit depredations on their property, disturb the peace by threats or otherwise, or commit other overt acts of hostility, we recommend the employment of sufficient force to bring them into subjection, and to place them upon the Nez Percés Reservation. The Indian agent at Lapwai should be fully instructed to carry into execution these suggestions, relying at all times upon the department commander for aid when necessary."

Now, there was nothing like precipitancy in all this; so that the wonderfully abrupt advent of General Howard, with a fear of the laughter of the white man in his heart, and a threat of violence on his tongue, is all fiction.

Doubtless Joseph was told that the commission had

recommended "that Wallowa should be held by military occupation," to *prevent* and not to make war, and that I should have the work to do.

This commissioner's report was approved at Washington. The Indian Agent, Mr. Monteith, did all that lay in his power to carry out the recommendations at first without military aid.

The Indians called me to an interview first at Walla Walla, afterward at Lapwai. At Walla Walla the talk with Joseph's brother Ollicut was exceedingly pleasant. I write of it, "The old medicine-man looks happy, and Ollicut believes we shall have no trouble. . . .

"I made the appointment for Lapwai in twelve days, but I went to Lewiston immediately to meet the officers of Fort Lapwai, and Indian Agent Monteith, to read to them carefully the full instructions from the Honorable Secretary of War, General Sherman, and the commanding general of the military division, in relation especially to the agency the military was to have in placing the Indians upon the reservation."

I made a visit to Wallula and then returned by stage to meet the non-treaties at Lapwai the 3rd of May (1877). This is the council to which Joseph invited me, and not I him, as he alleges.

Before giving points in this interview in answer to Joseph's statements, I must state that Mr. Monteith, Indian Agent, had been instructed by his chief at Washington, to bring the "non-treaty Nez Percés" upon their reservation. He had made his official demand upon me. I had been positively ordered to give the essential aid. There was now nothing left to parley about, yet to please the Indians I had promised to meet them again, and I did.

These picturesque people came in sight, after keeping

us waiting long enough for effect. They drew near the hollow square of the post and in sight of us, the small company to be interviewed. They struck up their song. They were not armed except with a few "tomahawk-pipes" that could be smoked with the peaceful tobacco or penetrate the skull-bone of an enemy, at the will of the holder"; yet, somehow, this wild song produces a strange effect. Our ladies, thinking it a war-song, ask with some show of trepidation, "Do you think Joseph means to fight?" The Indians sweep around the fence and make the entire circuit, still keeping up the song as they ride, the buildings breaking the refrain into irregular bubblings of sound till the ceremony was completed.

After all had finally gathered at the tent, and Father Cataldo had opened by a prayer in the Nez Percés language, I turned to Joseph and said through Mr. Whitman (the interpreter): "I heard from your brother Ollicut, twelve days ago at Walla Walla, that you wished to see me. I am now here to listen to what you have to say."

Joseph then told me of other Indians coming and said, "You must not be in a hurry to go till all get in, to have a talk."

I replied: "Mr. Monteith, the Indian Agent, and I have our instructions from Washington. They send us to your people. If you decide at once to comply with the wishes of the Government, you can have the first pick of vacant land. We will wait for White Bird if you desire it. Instructions to him are the same as to you. He can have his turn." And an old Dreamer intimating that they wished a long talk, the answer is: "Mr. Monteith and I wished to hear what you have to say, whatever time it may take; but you may as well know at the outset that, in any event, the Indians must obey the orders of the Government of the United States."

Mr. Monteith then read his instructions from the Indian Bureau to the Indians and had them carefully interpreted to them, and also explained how he had already informed them of the orders to come on the reservation through Reuben (then head-chief at Lapwai) and that they had scorned his message. "Now, you *must* come, and there is no getting out of it. Your Indians, and White Bird's, can pick up your horses and cattle and come on the reservation. . . . General Howard will stay till matters are settled."

Ollicut replied at length, objecting to considering matters settled.

I rejoined: "Joseph, the agent, Mr. Monteith, and myself are under the same Government. What it commands us to do, that we must do. The Indians are to come on the reservation first; *then* they may have privileges, as the agent has shown, to hunt and to fish in the Imnaha Valley. If the Indians hesitate to come to the reservation, the Government directs that soldiers be used to bring them hither. Joseph and Ollicut know that we are friends to them, and that if they comply there will be no trouble."

Everybody at this council was in good humor, except two old Dreamers who tried to make a disturbance. I told them pointedly to give good advice. My manner I will not judge of. It is my usual manner, proceeding from the kindest of feelings, and from an endeavor to behave as a gentleman to the weakest or most ignorant human being. The Indians, excepting the two I have named, made no angry remarks. We shook hands and separated, to wait as Joseph had requested.

Joseph has turned this right about in the article

published in the *Review* where it is stated that he said, "I am ready to talk to-day," and that General Howard would not. His account runs two days' interviews into one. Joseph never made that interesting speech ending with "I do not believe that the Great Spirit Chief gave one kind of men the right to tell another kind of men what they must do." And I did never reply, "You want to dictate to me, do you?" We always treated each other with the most marked courtesy.

On May 4th Joseph made a brief speech: "This is White Bird; I spoke to you of him; this is the first time he has seen you and you him. I want him and his Indians to understand what has been said to us."

White Bird was a demure-looking Indian, about five feet eight inches in height. His face assumed the condition of impassability while in council; he kept his ceremonial hat on, and placed a large eagle's wing in front of his eyes and nose.

The sub-chief and Dreamer, Too-hool-hool-suit, was broad-shouldered, deep-chested, five feet ten in height, had a deep guttural voice, and betrayed in every word a strong and settled hatred of all Caucasians. This man the Indians now put forward to speak for them — not that they had already decided to indorse his sentiments, but because he always counseled war; they evidently desired to see what effect his public utterance would produce upon us.

Now, instead of the mild and respectful speech attributed to this surly Indian by Joseph, a speech that was followed by my causeless loss of temper, Mr. Monteith and I heard him patiently, for quite a length of time, asserting his independence and uttering rebellious speeches against the Washington authority. We replied firmly and kindly as before, explaining everything and showing the imperative nature of our instructions.

The White Bird Indians were very tired that day, and Joseph again asked for delay. The record reads: "Let the Indians take time; let them wait till Monday morning, and meanwhile talk among themselves. So, with pleasant faces and cordial handshaking, the second interview broke up."

How different this is from Joseph's account of the affair, in which he condenses the whole narrative into the arrest of Too-hool-hool-suit upon his first appearance, and without provocation.

Now (Monday, May 7th), we came together again. The "non-treaties" had received large accessions. The display (previous to seating themselves) gave them great boldness. Our garrison was but a handful, and the manner of the Indians was now defiant. Mr. Monteith began in the kindest manner to show the Indians that their religion would not be interfered with, nor their ceremonies, unless the peace was disturbed by excessive drumming.

Then Too-hool-hool-suit began in the most offensive style. We listened to the oft-repeated Dreamer nonsense with no impatience, till finally he accused us of speaking untruthfully about the chieftainship of the earth.

I thought the time had come to check his tirade. I was not in the least angry, if I recall my mood with accuracy; I did not lose my temper, but I did assume a severity of tone sufficient to show that I understood the drift of the council, and that we were not to be intimidated. My first words were: "I do not want to interfere with your religion, but you must talk about practicable things. Twenty times over I hear that the earth is your mother, and about the chieftainship of the earth; I want to hear it no more, but to come to business at once."

He then talked against the treaty Indians, and said they had no law, or their law was born of to-day; then against us white people for attempting to divide the earth, and defiantly asking, "What do you mean?"

Mr. Monteith explained: "The law is, you must come to the reservation. The law is made in Washington; we don't make it." Then, again, the Dreamer goes over the same ground and becomes fiercer and fiercer. The crowd of Indians are becoming excited, and I saw that I must act, and that very promptly. The record is: "The rough old fellow, in his most provoking tone, says something in a short sentence, looking fiercely at me. The interpreter quickly says: 'He demands what person pretends to divide the land and put me on it?' In the most decided voice I said: 'I am the man; I stand here for the President, and there is no spirit, good or bad, that will hinder me. My orders are plain and will be executed. I hoped that the Indians had good sense enough to make me their friend and not their enemy.'"

From various unmistakable signs (1 am no novice with Indians) I saw that immediate trouble was at hand. Joseph, White Bird, and Looking Glass indorsed and encouraged this malcontent. I must somehow put a wedge between them; so I turned to this Dreamer and said, "Then you do not propose to comply with the orders of the Government?"

After considerable more growling and impudence of manner, he answered with additional fierceness, "The Indians may do what they like, but I am not going on the reservation." After telling the Indians that this bad advice would be their ruin, I asked the chiefs to go with me to look at their land. "The old man shall not go. I will leave him with Colonel Perry." He says, "Do you want to scare me with reference to my body?" I said, "I will leave your body with Colonel Perry." I then arose and led him out of the council, and gave him in charge of Colonel Perry.

The whole tone of the Indians now changed, and they readily agreed to go with me to look at their new homes. They may have thought of killing me then and there; but a bold, quick, unexpected action will often save you in extreme peril. Joseph's manner was never defiant. He rode with me to look at what Mr. Monteith had intended for him. A few Indians and some white sojourners would have to remove to other lands, to put Joseph's people together. We lunched together at Mr. Colwell's and then returned to the fort. White Bird and Looking Glass appeared to be happy and contented. They pleaded for the release of Too-hool-hool-suit; but I told them to wait until I had shown them their land which Mr. Monteith would designate. The next day we rode to Kamiah (sixty-five miles), and the next went to the lands intended. White Bird picked his near Looking Glass's farms, and then we returned to Kamiah, and the next day following to Lapwai.

Too-hool-hool-suit was released on the pledge of Looking Glass and White Bird, and on his earnest promise to behave better and give good advice.

Now we must have our final interview, May 14th. Joseph concluded to go, too, near Kamiah with the rest. The promises were put in writing. No objection was made to thirty days, except by Hush-hush-cute. I gave him thirty-five days because he had not had so early notice of removal.

I withheld the protection papers from Hush-hush-cute because of something he said, which indicated that he was attempting to conceal his intentions. So I left his papers with the agent. There was general joy among the treaty Indians, non-treaty Indians, and whites, at the peaceful outcome of the councils, and I returned to Portland.

This idea that General Howard caused the war is an after-thought.

That story that Joseph asked me for more time is not true. That I sent orders to the soldiers to drive them out on their return to Wallowa is, of course, untrue; that would have disconcerted everything; on the contrary, the officers and soldiers were simply to occupy Wallowa in the interest of peace, and not use constraint unless forced to do so.

The statements with reference to our losses and those of the Indians are all wrong, and Joseph does not tell how his own Indians, White Bird and his followers, who treacherously escaped, after the terms of the surrender had been agreed upon between us at General Miles' battle-field, being permitted by himself, did in fact utterly break and make void the said terms of surrender.

These Indians were to return to Idaho, not because of any promise, but because of General McDowell's orders, requiring all the Nez Percé prisoners to be kept in my department. This order was changed by General Sherman, or at Washington.

This is the end of this publication.

Any remaining blank pages are for our book binding requirements and are blank on purpose.

To search thousands of interesting publications like this one, please remember to visit our website at:

http://www.kessinger.net

Printed in the United Kingdom
by Lightning Source UK Ltd.
118803UK00001B/115